Celebrations Around the World

LEVEL 9

DEC○DABLES
BY jump!

Teaching Tips

Gold Level 9

This book focuses on developing reading independence, fluency, and comprehension.

Before Reading

- Ask readers what they think the book will be about based on the title. Have them support their answer.

Read the Book

- Encourage readers to read silently on their own.
- As readers encounter unfamiliar words, ask them to look for context clues to see if they can figure out what the words mean. Encourage them to locate boldfaced words in the glossary and ask questions to clarify the meaning of new vocabulary.
- Allow readers time to absorb the text and think about each chapter.
- Ask readers to write down any questions they have about the book's content.

After Reading

- Ask readers to summarize the book.
- Encourage them to point out anything they did not understand and ask questions.
- Ask readers to review the questions on page 23. Have them go back through the book to find answers. Have them write their answers on a separate sheet of paper.

© 2024 Booklife Publishing
This edition is published by arrangement with Booklife Publishing.

North American adaptations © 2024 Jump!
5357 Penn Avenue South
Minneapolis, MN 55419
www.jumplibrary.com

Library of Congress Cataloging-in-Publication Data is available at www.loc.gov or upon request from the publisher.

ISBN: 979-8-88996-912-9 (hardcover)
ISBN: 979-8-88996-913-6 (paperback)
ISBN: 979-8-88996-914-3 (ebook)

Photo Credits

Images are courtesy of Shutterstock.com. With thanks to Getty Images, Thinkstock Photo and iStockphoto. Cover – Yuganov Konstantin. p4–5 – IVASHstudio, rozbyshaka. p6–7 – MIA Studio, Teo Wei Keong. p8–9 – Cait Eire, pics721. p10–11 – Drazen Zigic, niranana. p12–13 – SMDSS, StockImageFactory.com. p14–15 – AGCuesta, Hugo Brizard - YouGoPhoto. p16–17 – digidreamgrafix, LightField Studios. p18–19 – blueeyes, Golden Pixels LLC. p20–21 – Inara Prusakova, Rimma Bondarenko.

Table of Contents

Page 4   What Are Celebrations?

Page 6   Chinese New Year

Page 8   St. Patrick's Day

Page 10   Ramadan

Page 12   Diwali

Page 14   Day of the Dead

Page 16   Thanksgiving

Page 18   Hanukkah

Page 20   Christmas

Page 22   Index

Page 23   Questions

Page 24   Glossary

What Are Celebrations?

Celebrations are times when people come together to mark special events. There are many different types of celebrations. Some celebrations can be part of a person's religion, a country's history, or part of family life.

People use celebrations to give thanks and show what is important to them and their **culture**. For some celebrations, people might have certain **customs**, eat certain foods, wear special clothing, or listen to a certain type of music.

Chinese New Year

Chinese New Year or Lunar New Year is celebrated by Chinese people all over the world. The celebrations often last many weeks. On Lunar New Year's Eve, children are given money in red envelopes as a gift.

Families often celebrate Lunar New Year with a big meal and by staying up very late. On New Year's Day, they celebrate with fireworks and parades. The parades often include fancy clothing, dancing, **acrobatics**, and drums.

St. Patrick's Day

Some countries have national days named after saints. Saints are people who are believed to be very good. Saint Patrick is the **patron saint** of Ireland. Every year on March 17, people in Ireland celebrate St. Patrick's Day.

St. Patrick's Day is celebrated in many countries across the world. People use this day to celebrate Irish culture. St. Patrick's Day is celebrated with parades.

The Chicago River in Chicago, Illinois, is dyed green for St. Patrick's Day.

Ramadan

Ramadan takes place over a whole month. It is a very important time for Muslims all over the world. During Ramadan, Muslims do not eat anything during daylight hours. This is called fasting. Once the sun sets, families eat big meals together.

Muslims use the month of Ramadan to focus on their religion, Islam. It helps them feel closer to their religion and their loved ones. Many Muslims also raise money or **donate** supplies to other people during Ramadan.

Diwali

Diwali is a five-day celebration also known as the Festival of Lights. It is celebrated by Hindus, Jains, and Sikhs all over the world. The Diwali story is different in different places, but it always celebrates good winning over evil.

During Diwali, people light small oil lamps. These lamps are used to invite the goddess of good fortune, Lakshmi, into their homes. People also use colorful powder or sand to make patterns called rangoli.

Rangoli

Day of the Dead

Day of the Dead is a festival that takes place every year in Mexico and other countries, including Spain and Brazil. This festival celebrates the lives of people who have died. People use it to remember their loved ones.

People set up small **altars** called ofrendas in their homes. These altars are decorated with photographs, candles, marigolds, and sugar skulls. During the festival, people often dress up and wear skull masks or makeup.

Marigolds

Photographs

Sugar skulls

Candles

Thanksgiving

On the third Thursday of November, many Americans celebrate Thanksgiving. On Thanksgiving, people gather with their families and celebrate with a meal. Many families use this time to think about the things they are grateful for.

Many families also use Thanksgiving to help other people by volunteering or donating food. Thanksgiving is often celebrated with a big parade that includes marching bands, floats, and musical performances.

Hanukkah

Hanukkah is a religious festival celebrated by Jewish people. The festival celebrates a miracle that happened long ago. A lamp that only had enough oil to last one day stayed lit for eight days. Therefore, Hanukkah lasts eight days.

During Hanukkah, Jewish people celebrate using a menorah. The menorah holds nine candles. A different candle is lit each evening of Hanukkah. There is one candle for every day that the lamp from the miracle burned. The ninth candle is used to light the rest.

Christmas

Christmas is celebrated in many ways in different places. In the United States, people give presents and eat Christmas dinner on December 25.
In other countries, including Norway, Denmark, and Sweden, these things happen on December 24.

Many different foods are eaten around the world at Christmas. In Denmark, people eat rice pudding with a whole almond hidden inside. Whoever finds the almond gets a gift.

In Italy, people bake a type of bread called panettone.

Index

candles 15, 19
family 4, 7, 10, 16–17
festivals 12, 14–15, 18
parades 7, 9, 17
religion 4, 11, 18

How to Use an Index

An index helps us find information in a book. Each word has a set of page numbers. These page numbers are where you can find information about that word.

Page numbers

Example: balloons 5, <u>8–10</u>, 19

Important word

This means page 8, page 10, and all the pages in between. Here, it means pages 8, 9, and 10.

Questions

1. What are some different types of celebrations?

2. Which religion celebrates Ramadan?

3. In Norway, when do families open Christmas presents?

4. Using the Table of Contents, can you find which page you can read about St. Patrick's Day?

5. Using the Index, can you find a page in the book about parades?

6. Using the Glossary, can you define what altars are?

Glossary

acrobatics:
Complex movements that require a lot of agility.

altars:
Raised areas on which people make offerings.

culture:
The beliefs and practices of a specific group of people.

customs:
Traditional ways of behaving.

donate:
To give to a charity to help others.

patron saint:
A saint who protects and guides people.